This book belongs to Mrs Smith

# To Eat Or Not To Eat?

## The Meat And Beans Group - Food Pyramid

## (2nd Grade Science Series)

**SPEEDY PUBLISHING**

Speedy Publishing LLC
40 E. Main St. #1156
Newark, DE 19711
www.speedypublishing.com

Copyright 2015

All Rights reserved. No part of this book may be reproduced or used in any way or form or by any means whether electronic or mechanical, this means that you cannot record or photocopy any material ideas or tips that are provided in this book

The meat and beans food group is also called the protein foods group.

The group is consists of meat, fish, poultry, nuts, seeds, eggs and dried beans.

They are grouped together since they are all good sources of dietary protein.

The meat group is one of the major compacted food groups in the food guide pyramid.

For those who do not consume meat or animal products, they can also eat the MEAT ALTERNATIVES.

The food guide pyramid suggests that adults eat 2-3 servings per day.

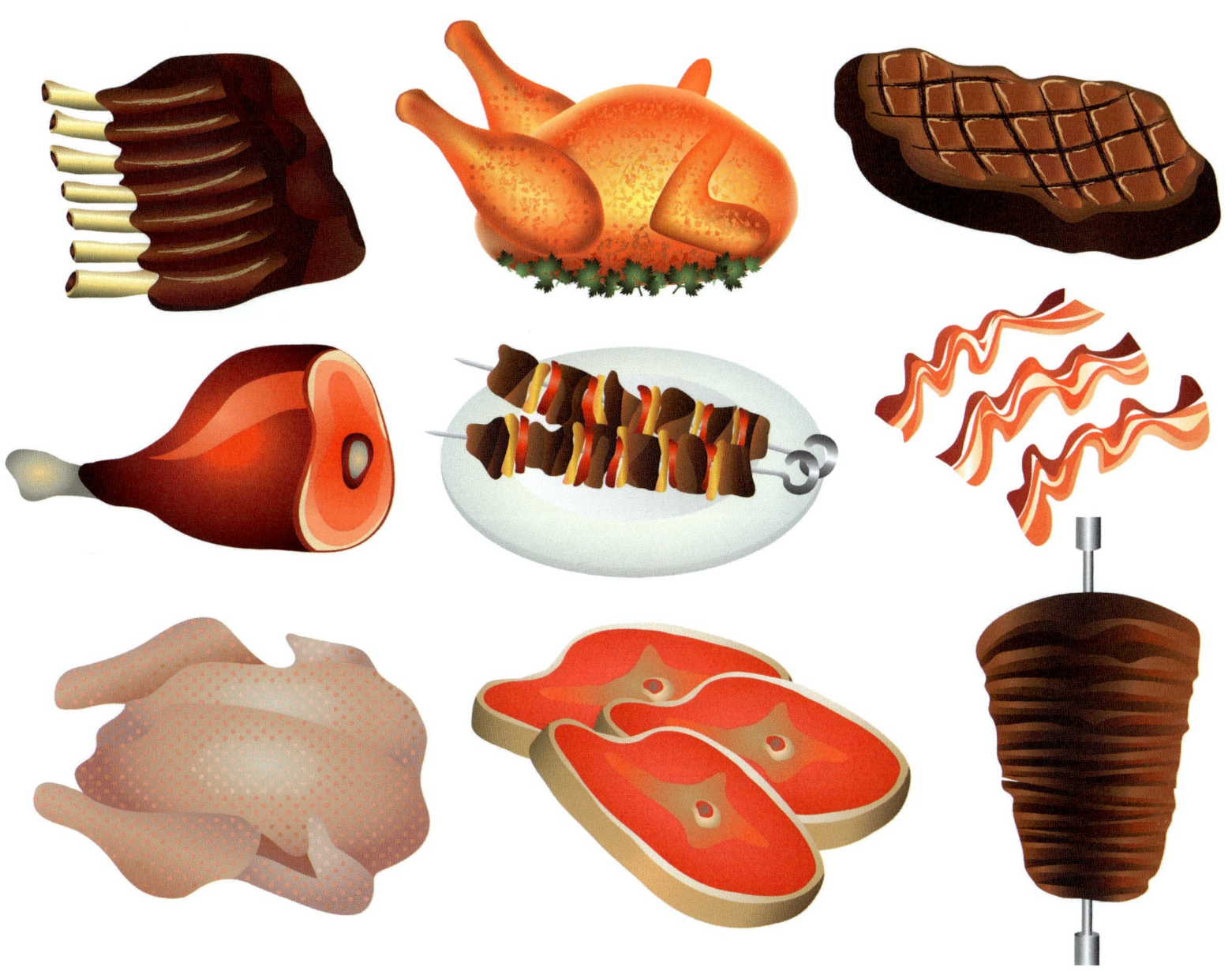

The healthy proteins in meat and beans function as building blocks for bones, muscles, cartilage, skin and blood.

Nuts and seeds are excellent sources of essential fatty acids and vitamin E.

Vitamin B12 is needed for healthy blood. It is found only in animal products.

You get essential amino acids from foods like meat, fish, eggs and milk.

Your body can not store protein, so you need to eat protein foods every day.

Even foods like peanut butter have protein but remember they have a lot of fat and some sugar as well!

Always try to choose meat, poultry and fish products that are low in fat when it is possible.

All the foods in this group provide B vitamins, which help with nervous system function, red blood cell formation and tissue repair.

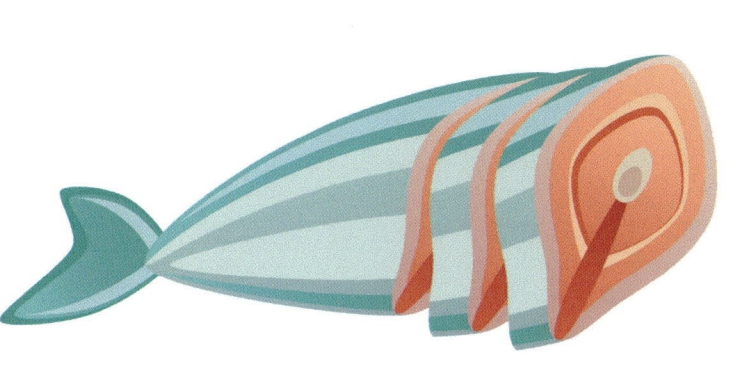

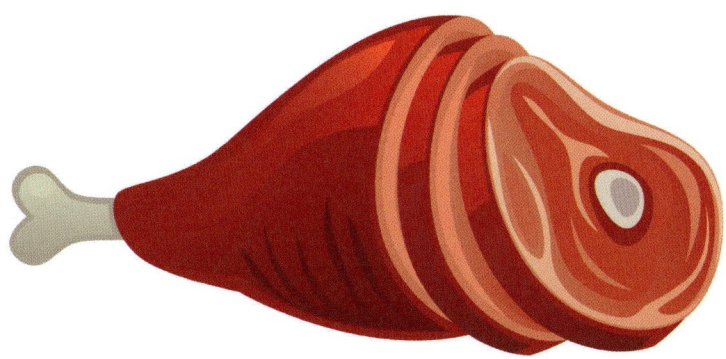

# Circle the pizza topping that is part of the meat and beans group

# Circle the food that is part of the meat and beans group

Printed in Great Britain
by Amazon